D0926481

DISCARD

SPEED MACHINES

ALFA ROMEO

Julia J. Quinlan

PowerKiDS
press

New York

PUBLIC LIBRARY
EAST ORANGE, NEW JERSEY

j 629.222
QUI

Published in 2013 by The Rosen Publishing Group, Inc.
29 East 21st Street, New York, NY 10010

Copyright © 2013 by The Rosen Publishing Group, Inc.

All rights reserved. No part of this book may be reproduced in any form without permission in writing from the publisher, except by a reviewer.

First Edition

Editor: Jennifer Way
Book Design: Greg Tucker

Photo Credits: Cover, p. 11 © www.iStockphoto.com/Marin Tomas; p. 4 Fedor Selivanov/Shutterstock.com; p. 5 Reg Lancaster/Hulton Archive/Getty Images; p. 6 Tom Burnside/Photo Researchers/Getty Images; p. 7 KENCKOphotography/ Shutterstock.com; pp. 8, 9, 17 (right) Car Culture/Getty Images; pp. 10, 19 Bloomberg/Getty Images; p. 12 Max Earey/ Shutterstock.com; p. 13 Julie Lucht/Shutterstock.com; pp. 14, 15 Bryn Lennon/Getty Images; p. 16 tratong/Shutterstock. com; p. 17 (top) Tungphoto/Shutterstock.com; pp. 18, 23 © Hans Dieter Seufert/c/age fotostock; p. 20 Foto011/ Shutterstock.com; p. 21 Biggi Braun/Getty Images; p. 22 Dikiiy/Shutterstock.com; pp. 24–25 Giuseppe Cacace/AFP/Getty Images; pp. 26, 27 © www.iStockphoto.com/Sjoerd van der Wal; pp. 28–29 ChinaFotoPress/Getty Images.

Library of Congress Cataloging-in-Publication Data

Quinlan, Julia J.
  Alfa Romeo / by Julia J. Quinlan. — 1st ed.
      p. cm. — (Speed machines)
  Includes index.
  ISBN 978-1-4488-7461-3 (library binding) — ISBN 978-1-4488-7533-7 (pbk.) —
ISBN 978-1-4488-7608-2 (6-pack)
  1. Alfa Romeo automobile—Juvenile literature. I. Title.
  TL215.A35Q55 2013
  629.222—dc23
                                2012007211

Manufactured in the United States of America

CPSIA Compliance Information: Batch #B4S12PK: For Further Information contact Rosen Publishing, New York, New York at 1-800-237-9932

$ 25.25
2/14/13
2B

i 13899624

Contents

Introducing Alfa Romeo   4

Italian Beginnings   6

Classic Designs   8

Today's Alfa Romeos   10

Racecars   12

Alfa Romeo Racing   14

Spider   16

Brera   18

Giulietta   20

8C Competizione   22

MiTo   24

159   26

The Future of Alfa Romeo   28

Comparing Alfa Romeos   30

Glossary   31

Index   32

Websites   32

Introducing Alfa Romeo

Alfa Romeo is an Italian company known for making luxury sports cars. Alfa Romeo is one of the oldest and most successful sports carmakers in the world. The company was founded over 100 years ago, in 1910. Although the company has had its ups and downs, Alfa Romeo has stayed in business for so long because it constantly **innovates** its cars. This means that it makes changes to its cars to keep up with the latest technology.

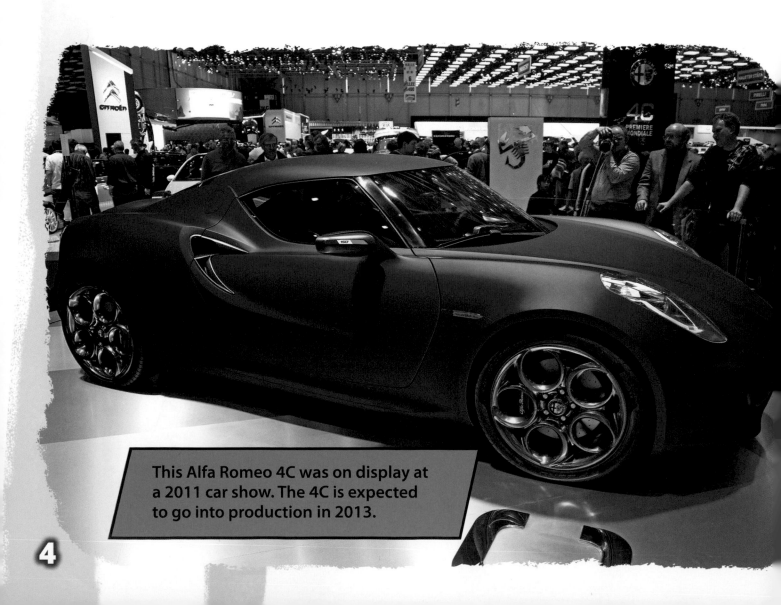

This Alfa Romeo 4C was on display at a 2011 car show. The 4C is expected to go into production in 2013.

Enzo Ferrari, shown here, once worked for Alfa Romeo. He founded his namesake company in 1929 and began producing Ferraris in 1947.

Alfa Romeo is not only **legendary** for its cars. It is also known for creating another legendary carmaker. It was the first company to employ Enzo Ferrari. Enzo Ferrari left the company and went on to create his own car company, Ferrari. Alfa Romeo is also known for its success in racing. The company has participated in several different races, and it has also built engines for other teams.

Italian Beginnings

Alfa Romeo began in 1910 as a company called ALFA located near Milan, Italy. In 1910, the company came out with its very first car, called the 24 HP. It had four **cylinders** and a top speed of 62 miles per hour (100 km/h). In 1911, ALFA created a racing version of the 24 HP, called the Corsa. This began the company's racing legacy. In 1920, ALFA changed its name to Alfa Romeo.

Here is a 1933 Alfa Romeo 8C 2600.

This 1953 Alfa Romeo 6C 3000 CM was used as a racecar.

Alfa Romeo began **exporting** cars to the United States in 1961. The first car to come to the United States was the Giulietta. Before Alfa Romeo exported its cars to the United States, a businessman and car lover named Max Hoffman **imported** them. Alfa Romeos were sold in the United States until 1995, when Alfa Romeo stopped exporting them there. However, Alfa Romeo plans to begin exporting cars to the United States again in 2013.

Classic Designs

Alfa Romeo, like many European sports car companies, began with a strong interest in racing. The company made its first racecar in 1913. Since that time, Alfa Romeo has competed in most types of car races. In fact, Alfa Romeo won the first ever Formula One World Championship in 1950!

The Spider has one of Alfa Romeo's most loved classic designs. This 1969 model was part of the Spider's first generation and is also known as the Duetto.

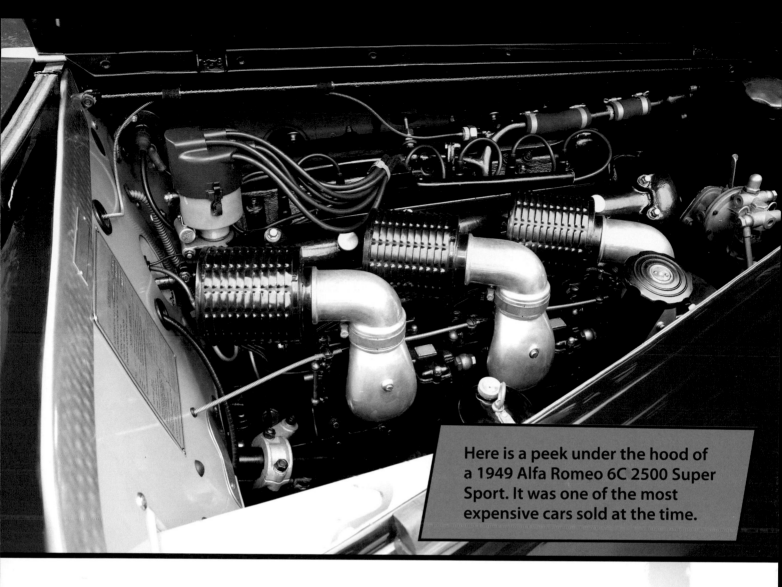

Here is a peek under the hood of a 1949 Alfa Romeo 6C 2500 Super Sport. It was one of the most expensive cars sold at the time.

Over the years, Alfa Romeo created stylish sports cars. Many became known for their classic designs. Today's Alfa Romeos are designed for people who want the look, feel, and performance of a sports car but also want safety and comfort.

One design that appears on every Alfa Romeo is the company's logo. It is a circle that is split in half. On the left side is a red cross, and on the right side is a green serpent, or snake.

Today's Alfa Romeos

In 2012, Alfa Romeo made four different models. They were a small family car called the Giulietta, a **subcompact** called the MiTo, a **sedan** called the 159, and a sport wagon called the 159 SW. Most of the cars in Alfa Romeo's 2012 lineup are very practical. This means that they are safe and have seating for more than one passenger and roomy trunks. Some models have **hatchbacks**, which are rear doors that make it easier to load things into the back of the car.

The MiTo, shown here, is a three-door subcompact car. A subcompact is a small car.

The Giulietta, shown here, is a small five-door hatchback. A hatchback has a rear door that opens upward.

Alfa Romeo is planning to introduce its first sport-utility vehicle, or SUV, in 2013. The SUV will be made to have good **fuel economy**. Fuel economy means that the car needs less gas to run, so drivers do not have to fill their tanks as often. This saves them money.

Racecars

Racecars are made specially for competing in racing competitions. They are made to be faster and to have more powerful engines. They are also not meant to be used for everyday driving.

The Zagato TZ3 Corsa, shown here, has an eight-cylinder engine and can reach a top speed of more than 186 miles per hour (300 km/h).

This Alfa Romeo is driving in a World Touring Car Championship race. A touring-car race uses production cars that have been changed for racing.

In 2010, the Alfa Romeo Zagato TZ3 Corsa was made in honor of the company's one-hundredth anniversary. A German collector **commissioned** this one-of-a-kind racecar. This means that the collector paid for the design and **production** of this car.

The Zagato TZ3 Corsa is based on a classic Alfa Romeo racecar called the Giulia TZ. The Giulia TZ was a racecar made by Alfa Romeo in 1963. It won several races in its first year, including Le Mans. Le Mans is the oldest **endurance** race for sports cars. The Giulia TZ had a four-cylinder engine and a top speed of 134 miles per hour (216 km/h).

Alfa Romeo Racing

Racing is very important for sports car companies. It gives them a chance to use the latest innovations in car making to build new cars. They can then show off their ability to create fast, powerful engines. Racing allows car companies to compete with each other and see which one is making the world's fastest racecars.

This Alfa Romeo is in a touring-car race. Touring cars do not go as fast as Formula One cars, but many fans prefer watching racecars that are based on production cars.

This Alfa Romeo is being raced in the World Touring Car Championship.

Alfa Romeo raced in Formula One races from 1950 until 1988. Formula One is a worldwide racing series that uses special single-seat racecars. Later it raced in Formula Three races. Formula Three uses the same type of cars as Formula One. People who want to become Formula One racers often begin their racing careers in Formula Three.

Alfa Romeo has competed in many types of races. It has raced in Formula Three races, rally races, and touring races such as the World Touring Car Championship.

Spider

The Spider is one of the most loved Alfa Romeos ever made. It was also the longest-running model of Alfa Romeo. It was made from 1966 until 1993. The Spider was designed by Pininfarina. Pininfarina is a famous Italian design company that has designed cars for Ferrari, Lamborghini, and many others.

The classic Spider is a convertible. "Spider" or "spyder" are common names for convertible sports cars. However, some models of the Alfa Romeo Spider were available as hardtops.

Here is a first-generation Spider. The first generation lasted from 1966 to 1969.

1966 Spider

Engine size	1.6 liters
Number of cylinders	4
Transmission	Manual (stick shift)
Gearbox	5 speeds
0–60 mph (0–97 km/h)	11.3 seconds
Top speed	115 mph (185 km/h)

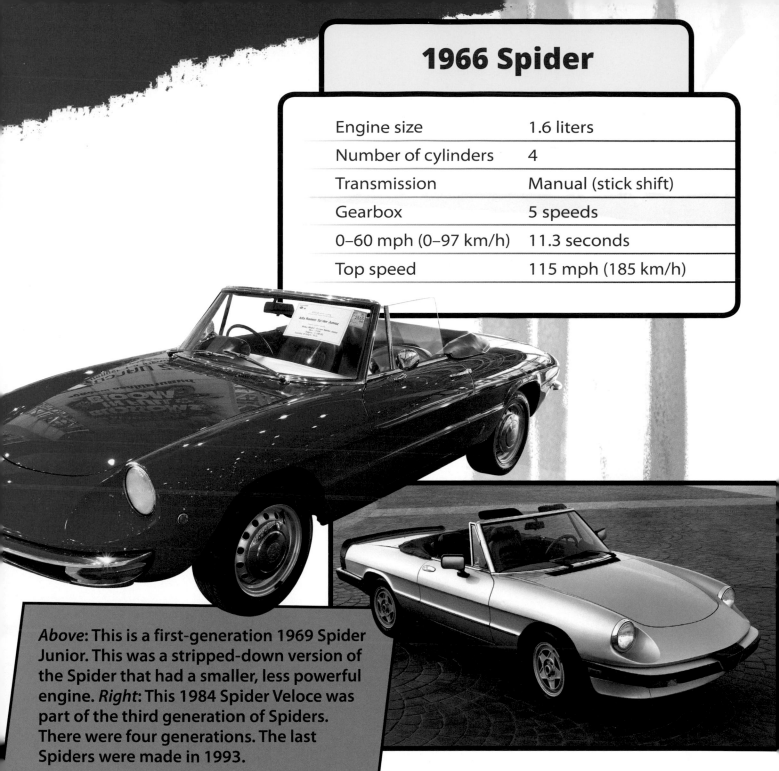

Above: This is a first-generation 1969 Spider Junior. This was a stripped-down version of the Spider that had a smaller, less powerful engine. *Right*: This 1984 Spider Veloce was part of the third generation of Spiders. There were four generations. The last Spiders were made in 1993.

The Spider was not only famous among car lovers, but it was also a movie star! It was famously featured in the 1967 movie *The Graduate*, which starred Dustin Hoffman. This car, a 1966 Spider, had a 1.6-liter engine with four inline cylinders. It had a top speed of 115 miles per hour (185 km/h) and a five-speed manual **transmission**.

Brera

The Alfa Romeo Brera was made from 2005 until 2010. Giorgetto Giugiaro of the Italdesign-Giugiaro car design and **engineering** company designed the Brera. There were two different styles of Breras. They were a coupe and a spider. The coupe was made from 2005 until 2010, and the spider was made from 2006 until 2010. The Brera was originally going to be Alfa Romeo's reintroduction into the US market. However, Alfa Romeo decided not to export the Brera.

Here is a Brera being driven on a test track. Although the Brera went out of production in 2010, there are rumors that the model will make a comeback in 2014.

2009 Brera Q4

Engine size	3.2 liters
Number of cylinders	6
Transmission	Manual or semiautomatic
Gearbox	6 speeds
0–60 mph (0–97 km/h)	6.8 seconds
Top speed	139 mph (224 km/h)

Over the course of its production, the Brera won several design honors, including the 2006 European Automotive Design Award.

The 2009 Brera Q4 had a 3.2-liter V6 engine and a six-speed manual transmission. It could go from 0 to 60 miles per hour (0–97 km/h) in 6.8 seconds. Its top speed was 139 miles per hour (224 km/h). The Brera Q4 had four-wheel drive. Four-wheel drive makes cars more manageable in difficult driving conditions, such as on wet roads.

Giulietta

The Alfa Romeo Giulietta was introduced in 2010. It replaced an earlier model, called the 147, and its design was based in part on one of Alfa Romeo's most popular models from the 1950s, the Giulietta Sprint Veloce. The current Alfa Romeo Giulietta is a five-door hatchback that was designed to be a stylish, small family car. This model was a big success for Alfa Romeo.

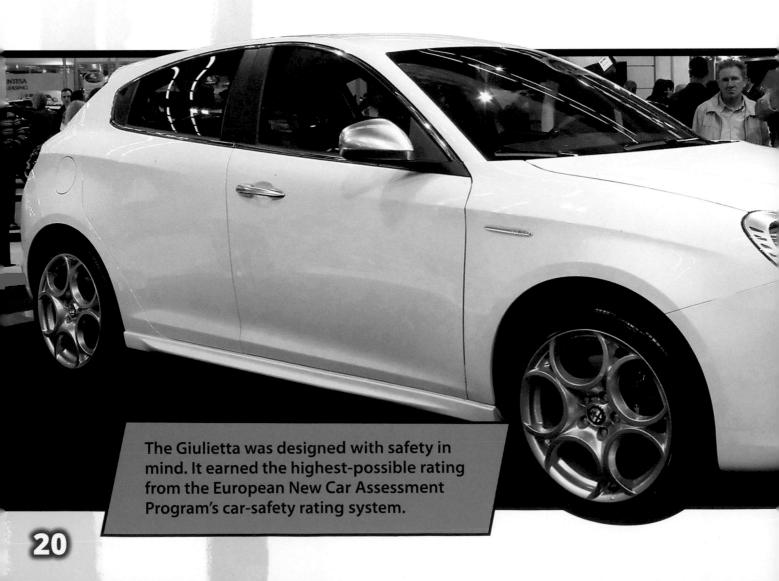

The Giulietta was designed with safety in mind. It earned the highest-possible rating from the European New Car Assessment Program's car-safety rating system.

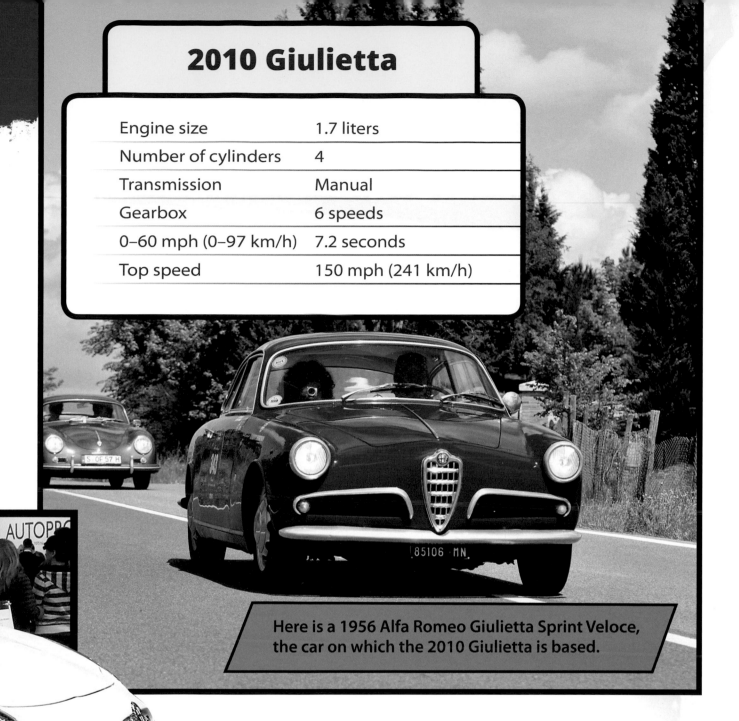

2010 Giulietta

Engine size	1.7 liters
Number of cylinders	4
Transmission	Manual
Gearbox	6 speeds
0–60 mph (0–97 km/h)	7.2 seconds
Top speed	150 mph (241 km/h)

Here is a 1956 Alfa Romeo Giulietta Sprint Veloce, the car on which the 2010 Giulietta is based.

The Giulietta was recognized for its quality as well as its popularity. It came in second in the 2011 Car of the Year awards. The Car of the Year awards are a European contest that has ranked cars every year since 1963. The 2010 Giulietta was yet another model that was rumored to be exported to the United States. Alfa Romeo eventually decided to push back its reentry into that market for a few more years.

8C Competizione

The 8C Competizione is named for its eight cylinders. This modern Alfa Romeo was designed to reflect the classic models of the 1950s and 1960s. There are two models of the Competizione. One is a two-door coupe. A coupe is a type of car with two doors and two seats. The coupe version of the Competizione was in production from 2007 until 2009. The other type of Competizione is a spider. A spider is a type of car that usually has a convertible top and two seats. The spider version of the Competizione was made from 2008 until 2010.

The concept version of the 8C Competizione spider was unveiled in 2005. The production version, shown here, was first shown at motor shows in 2008.

2007 8C Competizione

Engine size	4.7 liters
Number of cylinders	8
Transmission	Semiautomatic
Gearbox	6 speeds
0–60 mph (0–97 km/h)	4.2 seconds
Top speed	181 mph (291 km/h)

Here is a 2007 8C Competizione coupe. This car has a semiautomatic transmission. This means that the driver shifts the gears manually, but the clutch is controlled automatically.

The 2007 8C Competizione was a very fast and powerful car. It had a V8 engine. A V engine has its cylinders laid out in a V formation. The 8C was rare. Only 500 each of the coupe and the spider were made.

MiTo

The 2008 debut of the Alfa Romeo MiTo was a big change for Alfa Romeo. Alfa Romeo is known for its powerful sports cars, but the MiTo is a subcompact. A subcompact is a small road car made for city driving. The MiTo is considerably less powerful than most Alfa Romeos but is powerful compared to other cars in the subcompact class. The MiTo has a 1.4-liter engine and a top speed of 134 miles per hour (216 km/h). It can go from 0 to 60 miles per hour (0–97 km/h) in 8 seconds.

The MiTo was the first Alfa Romeo to have a DNA system. A DNA system has three different driving modes. They are called dynamic, normal, and all weather. That means that the driver can switch between driving modes depending on what the driving conditions are. For example, the all-weather mode is best for wet, slippery roads.

The name MiTo is a shortened form of the names of the Italian cities Milan and Turin, which is called Torino in Italian.

2012 MiTo

Engine size	1.4 liters
Number of cylinders	4
Transmission	Manual
Gearbox	6 speeds
0–62 mph (0–100 km/h)	8 seconds
Top speed	134 mph (216 km/h)

159

The Alfa Romeo 159 was made from 2005 until 2011. It came in two different styles, a four-door sedan and a five-door station wagon. The station wagon, called the 159 Sportwagon, was first shown at the 2006 Geneva Motor Show. The 2011 159 Sportwagon 2.0 JTDM was the last 159 station wagon. It has a six-speed manual transmission and front-wheel drive. Even though it is a family-friendly car, it also has the power for which Alfa Romeo is known.

From 2005 until 2010, the 159 was available with either a gasoline or a **diesel**-powered engine. In its final year, only diesel-powered

This is a sedan version of the final model year of the 159 at a 2012 car show.

2011 159 Sportwagon

Engine size	1.8 liters
Number of cylinders	4
Transmission	Manual
Gearbox	6 speeds
0–62 mph (0–100 km/h)	8.8 seconds
Top speed	136 mph (219 km/h)

Here is one of the final 159 Sportwagon models on display at a 2012 car show.

engines were produced. Diesel-powered engines tend to use less fuel in city driving than do gasoline-powered engines.

The 159 has also competed as a racecar. It came in first in its class in the 2009 Bathurst 12 Hour. The Bathurst 12 Hour is an endurance race that takes place near Bathurst, Australia.

The Future of Alfa Romeo

Alfa Romeo is a classic sports car brand. Although its cars have not been sold in the United States since 1995, car lovers still cannot wait for Alfa Romeo's return to America. Alfa Romeo could be back in the United States in 2013. In the meantime, collectors show their classic models at vintage car shows. Car lovers can also see the latest Alfa Romeo models displayed at car shows.

Alfa Romeo has remained successful and popular by having a wide range of cars. It does not focus only on sports cars that appeal only to serious car enthusiasts. It also makes cars for families and people who live in cities. There is an Alfa Romeo for everyone! All Alfa Romeo cars share the design and performance that made the company a legend.

People travel to car shows where they can see the latest Alfa Romeo concept cars and production models. This is a concept model at a 2011 car show in China.

Comparing Alfa Romeos

CAR	YEARS MADE	TRANSMISSION	TOP SPEED	FACT
Spider	1966–1993	5-speed manual	115 mph (185 km/h)	Duetto, the name for the first-generation Spider, was chosen by a write-in vote.
Brera	2005–2010	6-speed manual, 6-speed semiautomatic, or 6-speed automatic	139 mph (224 km/h)	*Autoweek* magazine chose the concept model for its Best in Show at the Geneva Motor Show.
Giulietta	2010–	6-speed manual	150 mph (241 km/h)	This model was voted Car of the Year in Greece in 2011.
8C Competizione	2007–2010	6-speed semiautomatic	181 mph (291 km/h)	*Competizione* is the Italian word for "competition."
MiTo	2008–	5-speed manual or 6-speed manual	134 mph (216 km/h)	The name MiTo is a play on the Italian word for "myth" or "legend."
159 Sportwagon	2005–	5-speed manual or 6-speed manual	136 mph (219 km/h)	The designer of the 159 is the same person who designed the Brera.

Glossary

commissioned (kuh-MIH-shund) Asked to do a job.

cylinders (SIH-len-derz) The enclosed spaces for pistons in an engine.

diesel (DEE-zel) A fuel used in engines.

endurance (en-DUR-ints) Strength and the ability to go long distances without breaking down.

engineering (en-juh-NEER-ing) Making and using technology.

exporting (ek-SPORT-ing) Sending something to another place to be sold.

fuel economy (FYOO-el ih-KAH-nuh-mee) A measurement of the distance traveled per amount of fuel used.

hatchbacks (HACH-baks) The backs of cars that open upward.

imported (im-PORT-ed) Brought in from another country for sale or use.

innovates (IH-nuh-vayts) Creates something new.

legendary (LEH-jen-der-ee) Famous and honored for a very long time.

production (pruh-DUK-shun) The method of making things.

sedan (sih-DAN) A car that seats four or more people.

subcompact (sub-KOM-pakt) A small car.

transmission (trans-MIH-shun) A group of parts that includes the gears for changing speeds and that conveys the power from the engine to the machine's rear wheel.

Index

C
carmaker(s), 4–5
car(s), 4–7, 9–11, 13–17,
    19–24, 26, 28, 30
collector(s), 13, 28
company, 4–6, 8, 14, 16,
    18, 28
Corsa, 6, 13
cylinders, 6, 17, 22–23

D
design(s), 9, 13, 20, 28

E
engine(s), 5, 12–14, 17, 19,
    23–24, 26–27

F
Ferrari, 5, 16

G
Giulietta, 7, 10, 20–21, 30

H
hatchback(s), 10, 20

M
MiTo, 10, 24, 30
model(s), 10, 16, 20–22,
    28, 30

N
name(s), 6, 16, 30

O
159, 10, 26–27, 30

P
performance, 9, 28
production, 13, 22

R
racecar(s), 8, 12–15, 27
race(s), 5, 8, 13, 15, 27
racing, 5, 8, 14

S
sedan, 10, 26
speed, 6, 13, 17, 19, 24
subcompact, 10, 24
success, 5, 20

T
transmission, 17, 19, 26, 30
type(s), 8, 15, 22

U
United States, 7, 21, 28

V
version, 6, 22

Websites

Due to the changing nature of Internet links, PowerKids Press has developed an online list of websites related to the subject of this book. This site is updated regularly. Please use this link to access the list: www.powerkidslinks.com/alfa/